STELLAR INTERVIEW PERFORMANCE
GUIDE TO ACE INTERVIEWS

VINOD JOSHI

INDIA • SINGAPORE • MALAYSIA

Notion Press

Old No. 38, New No. 6
McNichols Road, Chetpet
Chennai - 600 031

First Published by Notion Press 2019
Copyright © Vinod Joshi 2019
All Rights Reserved.

ISBN 978-1-64324-664-2

This book has been published with all efforts taken to make the material error-free after the consent of the author. However, the author and the publisher do not assume and hereby disclaim any liability to any party for any loss, damage, or disruption caused by errors or omissions, whether such errors or omissions result from negligence, accident, or any other cause.

No part of this book may be used, reproduced in any manner whatsoever without written permission from the author, except in the case of brief quotations embodied in critical articles and reviews.

THERE IS NO GREATER INVESTMENT THAN
CAREER IN A PERSON'S LIFE.

INTERVIEWS ARE THE GATEWAYS
TO A GREAT CAREER.

Contents

Preface 7
Acknowledgments 9

1. Interview Jitters 11
2. Hiring People 14
    Why Do Organizations Hire People? 14
    Why Are Interviews Necessary? 16
    Case Study – Ron Joins His New Job 18
3. Interviews – The Inner View 20
    What Do Employers Look for in an Interview? 20
    Ability 20
    Willingness 26
    Fit 27
4. Interviews – The Outer View 29
    Attire and Grooming 30
    Grooming Tips for Men 32
    Grooming Tips for Women 32
    Case Study – Nick and Tony 35
5. Communication 37
    The Importance of Listening 38

	Good vs. Effective Communication	39
	Non-Verbal Cues	42
6.	Applying for a Job	44
	Make a Great CV	44
	Covering Letter	45
	Documents and Certificates	45
	Appearance, Attire, and Grooming	46
	Case Study – XYZ Manufacturing	47
7.	The Preliminary Interview	49
	Telephone Interview	50
	Videoconference	51
	Case Study – Interview Planning	53
8.	The Final Interview	55
	Planning and Preparation	55
	Anticipating Interview Questions	59
	Social Media	62
9.	Handling the Final Interview	63
	The Interview Begins	64
	Handling Difficult Situations	68
	Group Discussion	70
	Post Interview Reflections	73
Annexure 1	Behavioral Interview Questions	77
Annexure 2	Interview Planning and Preparation Checklist	86

Preface

The idea of this book has been in my mind for a long time. In my career as a consultant and facilitator to organizations, and as a panelist interviewing potential employees, I observe that many candidates have all the education, experience and background necessary to perform the jobs they apply for, but are unable to make a positive impression during the interview. I believe this is because many job seekers do not have a structured approach to prepare for interviews. Even though our careers span a large part of our lifetimes, job interview situations arise only a handful of times, and the challenges interviews present become more significant with age, experience, responsibilities and compensation expectations.

The right to work is universal. It means finding employment in an organization, and most of us do want to work in an organization of our choice. Such organizations have a very well-defined and structured method to assess our suitability; therefore, understanding the interview process and preparing for it is crucial for success.

I have seen over and over again, that candidates who get selected for jobs are the ones who are ready with their answers. Their CVs/resumes are immaculate; they not only have great abilities, knowledge, and experience but are also well-prepared for interviews and hence, they stand apart.

In contrast, very knowledgeable and experienced individuals often fail miserably at interviews as they are not prepared, and are unable to demonstrate skills which would guarantee them success. Their disappointment becomes acute when such failures get repeated. After experiencing such lost opportunities multiple times, many job seekers become frustrated and lose confidence. They become stuck and are unable to make progress in their careers.

This book has been written to help individuals at any stage of their careers to prepare for job interviews so they can succeed at getting the jobs they desire. You maybe twenty-five years old or fifty, woman or man, teacher or banker, straight out of college or a seasoned executive seeking a change of job. You may also be a parent returning to the workforce or a homemaker who wants to have additional income. By following the guidance in this book, and systematically planning and preparing for interviews, you will be able to present your best self to prospective employers.

I wish you all good luck.

Acknowledgments

The insights that are reflected in this book have come from thousands of professionals whom I have met either during my training programs or as a member of panels conducting job interviews.

I am thankful to all of you for the learning and knowledge I gained during my interactions. I may not remember all of you by name, but the memories are fresh.

I am very thankful to my wife Kalpana, who worked tirelessly with me during the process of writing this book. My thanks also go to my daughter Shruti for the significant contribution she made in putting this book together. Her knowledge and insights were precious in articulating my thoughts and my experiences in this book.

1
Interview Jitters

Do you get butterflies in your stomach, feel tongue-tied, have sweaty palms and a dry mouth when you are facing an interview?

Many people are nervous before and during interviews. When you are embarking on something so crucial for your future life, it is natural to be stressed. There is a lot at stake, and you and your loved ones have high expectations.

Interview jitters are experienced in different ways. Some physical symptoms are

- Heart thumping
- Feeling breathless or breathing fast
- Restlessness – moving and constantly fidgeting, unable to sit still
- Talking very fast
- Hands trembling
- Clumsiness-can't find what is needed, things falling out of hands
- Sleeplessness – tossing and turning in bed

You may feel jittery during the interview and think

- It was all a bad idea; I shouldn't have come to this interview
- I am not sure I will be able to utter a word
- I don't think anyone is listening to me
- I am blabbering. Nothing I say makes sense.
- I can't find my voice, and I am forgetting things
- If I look at the interviewer's faces, I won't be able to talk to them
- This interview is taking forever.
- How much longer will this go on?
- All these interviewers look so overpowering.
- "Oh God! Why did you put me in this position?"

Again, it is normal to feel this way, and the only way to manage these jitters is to make sure you are well prepared for the interview. With this book in your hands, you now have a companion that will help you navigate your journey through the interview process with readiness and confidence. I have distilled lessons I learned in 25 years as a corporate consultant and interviewer into easy to understand insights, concepts, and checklists that are sure to bring you success.

Initially, in Chapters 2 and 3, you will gain an understanding of why people get hired and what intrinsic qualities interviewers look for in job seekers. You can then use Chapters 4 and 5 to understand how appearance and communication skills play a crucial role in ensuring your success in interviews, and how you can improve these to the best of your potential. The remaining chapters 6, 7, 8 and 9 contain specific instructions for each step – from applying for a job to appearing for final in-person interviews – so you are ready for any challenges that come your way.

2
Hiring People

Why Do Organizations Hire People?

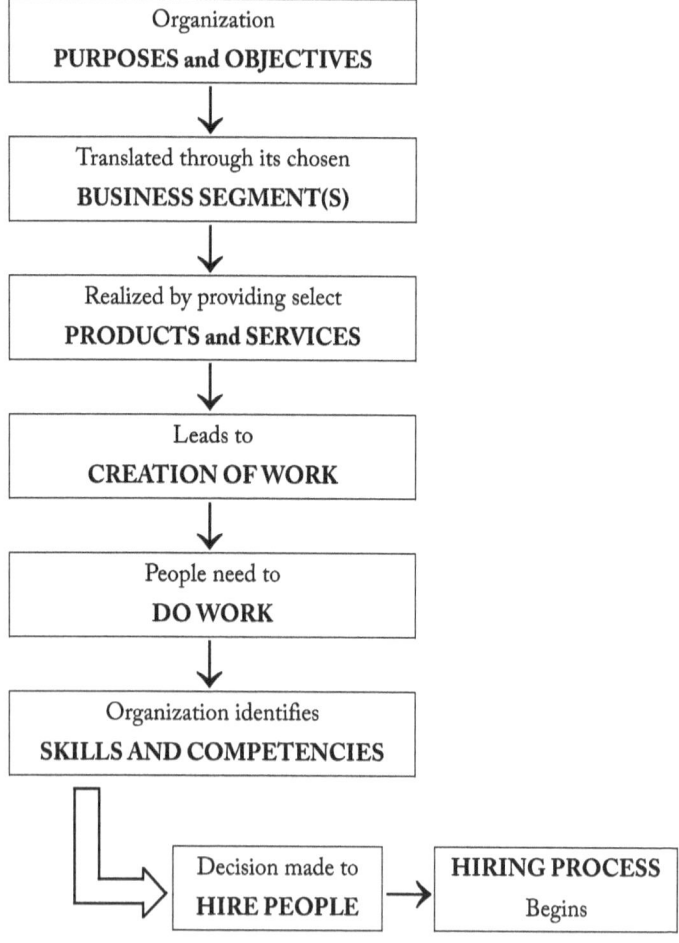

This cascade is a straightforward representation of the creation of jobs in organizations. In actual cases, the flow of these decisions may be much more complicated.

Once the need for hiring is determined, it is the responsibility of the people managing the hiring process to look out for and select people who will be most suitable for fulfilling the organization's purposes and objectives.

People – The Great Differentiator

What sets great organizations and successful businesses apart? Why do some companies thrive while others never get off the ground? Why are some organizations able to profoundly influence markets and society? Today companies like Tata, Amazon, Toyota, Apple, and Infosys are household names, and they touch every aspect of our lives. How did they get there? Ultimately, it all comes down to one thing – the people who work there.

Be it manufacturing a car, delivering pizza, managing stocks, or selling shoes; people are involved directly in each step of the process. How they do their jobs determines whether their organization thrives or fails.

Decisions about hiring people are the most important decisions that any organization has to make. While many other investments depreciate with time, the cost of employing people continuously rises. What differentiates excellent organizations from others is that they view employees as vital assets who become more valuable as they learn and grow.

People get hired at different levels in organizations to carry out various jobs, and the hiring process must take into account the differences in skills, knowledge, and experience required for different roles and duties. A manufacturing company may need engineers from several different specialties – civil engineers for building projects, software engineers for computer systems and mechanical engineers for design and production. The same manufacturing company also needs accountants, salespeople, customer service representatives and secretaries who all have different roles and responsibilities. Just as in a shopping mall, a store manager and a salesperson have different duties they have to perform.

The decisions involved in hiring employees can be very complex involving consideration of many factors; hence, the process of hiring can become a long-drawn one. Many people think the most critical factor is the cost of the employee to the organization; however, as we go further, you will see there are several other relevant considerations.

Why Are Interviews Necessary?

Employers have to choose between many individuals who have different and unique qualifications, experiences and talents and select one candidate that is the best fit for a specific set of roles and responsibilities of a particular job. The organization's present and future depend on the judgment of the people who hire employees. That is why individuals seeking employment are thoroughly evaluated by a hiring committee or panel for their potential to fulfill present and future job requirements.

Great care is taken at the time of hiring because once a person is employed, it places considerable responsibility on an organization to make sure the employee is engaged in constructive and profitable work. The method organizations use to perform this screening and evaluation process is the interview. Later in this book, we will take a look at the different facets of an interview, and why as a job seeker, it is critical to pay attention to and prepare for each stage of this process. For now, let's hear Ron's story.

Case Study – Ron Joins His New Job

Today was Ron's first day at his new role as the Executive Vice President in a multinational company. When Ron accepted this offer, at the age of 45, he thought that his career was now "all set"!

His new designation carried higher responsibilities, a very handsome remuneration package, and many great perks. The job came with a large office, secretarial and executive staff, membership in professional associations and clubs, an attractive entertainment allowance, and a holiday package for Ron and his family.

Ron spent his first day getting familiar with the organization, meeting his staff as well as completing joining formalities. In the evening, when he reached home, his wife Lily greeted him with a smile. Seeing him, she said "You seem very happy, Ron. I can see it on your face." His children asked, "How was your first day, Dad?"

The family sat down to chat. Ron gave them an overview of his job and the organization he is working for. He said, "Our Company is a very respectable organization having several divisions and business interests across the globe." He added, "It was my long-held dream to work in an organization like this; this puts my career on the fast track."

Jack, his son, excitedly said, "Dad, can I now get my new tennis racquet and shoes?" Ron smiled and said, "Sure." The family had put many purchases on hold until Ron found a new job with a higher salary. Lily softly smiled and said, "Ron, I will begin the search for our new home. Now we should be *able to pay a higher mortgage." Ron remembered that he and Lily had put buying a new house on hold. They needed a larger place as their children were growing up.*

The children went out to play while Ron and Lily continued to chat about the new job. Ron said, "I had wanted this change for quite some time, but every time I appeared for an interview with a reputed organization, I could never get what I wanted. This time the difference was that I prepared my career plan, decided the kind of organization I wanted to work for and took measures to understand the organizations I applied to in great detail. I even revised my CV to make sure that the profile I wanted to present was coming across clearly. I made a list of probable questions and practiced my answers and replies. I did not leave any stone unturned in my preparation for the interview."

Lily nodded in agreement and said, "Yes, I know you worked hard. You always had the potential, and this change happened when you began to take career planning seriously." Lily further said, "But don't forget the advice your friend gave you in preparing for your interview. That was crucial."

Ron very happily said, "Yes Lily, you're right, I am going to call him and say thank you. Because of him, we can now do all that we wanted; like making important investments in a new home, our retirement accounts, and our children's education. All the time that I put in planning my career and preparing for the interview was worth it."

Lily suddenly said, "Ron, is it not a fact that your career is the most important investment, as everything else follows it?"

3
Interviews – The Inner View

What Do Employers Look for in an Interview?

These are the two views you present during an interview.

- The inner view
- The outer view

The outer view is the view of how a person looks, behaves, and dresses. There are some fundamental aspects of the inner view, which the interviewers are seeking to find out in a short period. The crucial ones are as below.

Ability

Can this individual perform the tasks and duties the job requires?

Qualifications

To almost anyone reading this book, the meaning and importance of qualifications might already be apparent. Qualifications are the degrees and certificates you have received through formal education in secondary and post-secondary school systems, and courses you have completed in college at undergraduate and postgraduate levels.

Most employers look for a minimum level of credentials for every job. For instance, to be employed as an engineer or an architect one has to get a bachelor's degree from an accredited college.

In several countries, health care professionals such as surgeons, nurses, and physiotherapists have to pass national board exams to get licenses to practice in hospitals and clinics. Besides, many jobs require additional training and certification beyond school and college education. Flight attendants may have only a high school education, but they are required to complete specialized training and get a certificate for employment with an airline.

Knowledge

In today's world, knowledge acquisition happens through many different means – during formal education, seminars, workshops, and certification courses, through direct experience at doing things, from exposure to the Internet, books, and media, as well as interaction with people from various walks of life. Doctors gather knowledge not only from medical textbooks but also from other doctors that work with them in hospitals and by attending national and international conferences. Young lawyers get exposed to various aspects of litigation by serving as apprentices to older lawyers.

Take the example of a chef who works in a five-star hotel – he has a thorough understanding of ingredients and a finely-tuned palate that appreciates a diversity of flavors. He is also well versed in numerous cooking techniques, is familiar with the influence of culture on food, and is an expert at presenting food in a visually delightful way. This kind of depth and breadth of knowledge is fundamental to success in every profession.

In the interview context, knowledge and expertise get judged through questions for understanding how candidates improved performance in their work area. For example, a salesperson is asked how he used knowledge of the market in developing the company's market share. However, in some interviews, job seekers' learning is tested directly – software engineers are asked to write code, and a professor may be asked to deliver a lecture to college students. To get a job with a government organization in many countries, one has to take a formal examination.

There is another dimension used for assessing job-seekers' knowledge. The interview process probes candidates to understand how much effort they have made to know about the job they are seeking. If a candidate has no idea about an organization's products, services, market standing, and image, he will not fare as well as someone else who has studied the job description in detail, looked at the company's website, knows it products and services and has investigated how well the organization did in the past quarter or past year.

Skills

The interviewers try to gauge whether a candidate has the skills needed to tackle the responsibilities of the job on a day-to-day basis. In contrast with knowledge, which is abstract, skills are demonstrated through action and by producing tangible results. Take the instance of a carpenter – his knowledge may not be known to anyone until he uses manual skills of woodworking to build a piece of furniture. Nowadays, specific skills are universal; typical examples are computer literacy and telephone etiquette. Using the Internet, email software, and receiving and making phone calls are prerequisites for anyone who works in an office.

The skills required for a job depends on the level of the position in the hierarchical structure of an organization. Let us take a look at some examples. The skills that a teacher requires to manage a classroom full of 10-year old children are different from the skills a principal needs to have to run the school. Similarly, a line manager of a production unit in a factory must possess all the technical skills that his workers have. He must be thorough with the steps of the production process.

Additionally, he needs behavioral skills to motivate workers to do their best work. He must be adept at planning, scheduling, and coordination. He has, to ensure that the output meets the timelines as well as the specifications of quality. Such a manager should be proficient at managing time so he can attend to the multiple demands of his job.

For graduates fresh out of college who are not yet employed, effective communication skills are essential. Their leadership skills are evaluated based on extracurricular activities as a student.

Those seeking employment at senior levels get assessed for their leadership, team-building, facilitation skills, strategic thinking, and problem-solving abilities.

Experience

It is said that experience builds a person. The interviewers seek to understand a person's learning, application of knowledge and how the person utilized various skills to handle challenges and stressful situations. Their primary goal here is to judge how the candidates' experience and background may be relevant to the organization and which candidate will add the most value to the job they are hiring for.

Interviewers will often compare candidates' experiences from different angles. A comparison is made with other candidates on the number of years in the workforce, the duration of employment in the previous jobs and the time spent in various divisions in the organizations the candidate worked.

Candidates are also asked to describe projects in which they were involved, like improving processes and workflow, enhancing cost-effectiveness, improving quality, acquiring new markets and boosting productivity. Interviewers are likely to be very impressed by a candidate who made significant contributions like redesigning a product or service that was not doing well or achieved substantial increases in profitability, market share, and customer satisfaction.

An individual's experiences of working in collaboration with people at various levels are also critical. You may be asked to talk about how you guided new employees in learning the ropes and trained subordinates and peers on a new skill. The panel may take a keen interest when you discuss additional responsibilities your superiors entrusted to you because of your unique knowledge and skills, and how you delivered results within constraints of time and cost. Another accomplishment highly valued by interview panels is when a person sought and utilized feedback from buyers, team members and superiors to solve chronic problems in an organization's processes that led to increased customer satisfaction.

It is essential to remember that you are obligated to give a truthful account of your experiences and accomplishments. In today's world, no one achieves results alone, and many employees have a hand in successful projects and endeavors. Your credibility hinges on you taking credit for only your work and contributions. An authentic candidate earns the panel's respect and is much more likely to be hired.

Expertise

We need experts to perform activities that are difficult for everyone else to do. Experts get distinguished by highly specialized knowledge and skills they have in a particular field. Scientists, doctors, surgeons, psychologists, engineers, fashion designers, and mechanics can all be experts in their domains. Experts spend months, sometimes even years, learning, practicing and applying their knowledge and skills. They command respect because they can perform, create and deliver results with greater efficiency and effectiveness compared to other professionals from the same discipline. Are you an expert in a specific area? It can be your most significant selling point during an interview.

Willingness

Does this individual display readiness to take on the roles and responsibilities the job entails?

There are different aspects of willingness that interviewers look at. Some are assessed directly through questions that ask about your readiness to relocate, travel and work within a new reporting structure. Interviewers will also ask if you are ready to take on additional responsibilities beyond your current level of experience. Also, each organization has an established structure for compensation, and as you get closer to being selected for the job, the interviewers will look for your agreement with the salary scale the organization offers.

Certain aspects of willingness get gauged indirectly – interviewers may try to judge how keen you are to learn from the challenges presented to you by the new job and how adaptable you appear to the changing circumstances. The desire for learning is also assessed to determine whether a candidate is a good "fit" for a particular role. We will explore this later in this chapter.

Interviewers are also closely watching your body language, reactions, and listening to your tone. They look for people who demonstrate energy and enthusiasm for the new role and appear excited about working for their organization. Look at the chapter on communication to understand how you can display your willingness through clear and persuasive language and by presenting a positive demeanor during the interview.

Fit

Does this candidate genuinely belong in this role?

The nuances of how committees and panels select a person that is the "best fit" are the most obscure part of the interview process. Very often candidates wonder why they did not make the cut despite having all the right credentials and having given the correct answers to interview questions. This process has been made explicit below so that you can use these insights to prepare for interviews.

Firstly, fit is determined based on how easily a candidate can move into a new role. As we discussed in the previous section, candidates that appear enthusiastic and ready to take on what the job involves as well as those who are willing to relocate, travel and fulfill the requirements of the position are more likely to be hired.

During the interview, the committee tries to understand how distinctive and unique candidates are in comparison to each other. Often several candidates may have fared well during the interview process. The selection committee may engage in much debate on the advantages of hiring one candidate over others. They may discuss which individual might make the most significant contributions towards fulfilling the mission of the organization and whether a person's value system seems congruent with the environment of the organization.

Let's consider the issue of compensation and benefits. Most employers understand that making more money and moving up the ladder are essential goals for job seekers; however, they may not look favorably upon candidates that seem to be seeking employment with them only for increasing their compensation or for getting a lofty title. Irrespective of the industry, role or level, employers place a premium on values such as integrity, accountability, and transparency. They look for individuals who have a sense of commitment towards their work, want to excel in their roles, and demonstrate a work ethic which indicates that they can be relied upon to complete their responsibilities.

Other ways that interviewers try to select the best-fit person is by asking candidates to describe how they handled adverse situations with clients, conflicts between colleagues and sudden pressures of performance in their previous roles. No matter which industry you are seeking a job in, you will have to interact with people, and working on teams is required in almost all organizations today.

A candidate's communication skills and ability to collaborate with clients, superiors, peers and younger team members can be pivotal in the interviewer's assessment. It helps interviewers determine whether a particular individual will be able to maintain and facilitate a positive work culture in their organization.

Thorough preparation is your best bet to deal with this challenging aspect of interviews. Using the lists of questions and checklists in this book will help you gain clarity about your unique strengths and abilities, so you can confidently discuss with interviewers what makes you stand apart.

4
Interviews – The Outer View

For most people, the first impression of a new person gets formed rapidly and unconsciously. As soon as the person starts speaking, even if it's on the phone, our minds may immediately recognize specific attributes like the speaker's gender or accent. A person's facial expression and body language can reveal if he or she is upset, tired, happy or deep in thought. We also experience certain emotions when interacting with people; for example, you may feel disgusted if someone is wearing smelly socks, or get irritated if they talk very loudly.

During interviews, first impressions can matter a lot as candidates are immediately sized up within the first few moments of meeting the interviewers. The guidelines in this chapter are based on the many successful candidates I have met and what they did to prepare their appearance and demeanor in ways that avoided negative attention, and maintained the focus on their skills, abilities and fit for the job.

In my experience, many candidates arrived for interviews looking disheveled and unkempt. One candidate had his shirt collar turned up and the first two buttons of his shirt were wide open-he was judged as careless and disrespectful. Some candidates' choice of clothing was extremely flamboyant (fluorescent colors, animal prints) or poor fitting (jackets too small with buttons popping, or dresses that were too revealing). Some candidates reeked of smoke or body odor. Others came wearing loads of flashy jewelry and looked like they set out to attend a wedding, not an interview.

Also, many candidates did not pay attention to the type of job they were seeking. In specific industries, you may be in frequent contact with the media or may be directly interacting with customers and buyers. How you present yourself could impact the image of the organization and the customers' experience. It is especially important for marketing and sales professionals and in the hospitality industry. So, if you are looking to work as a server or concierge staff at a hotel, and you never smile, the interviewers may count that against you.

For some jobs, employees' appearance is essential – it may be OK for someone who is interviewing with a store that sells beauty products to have long, brightly painted fingernails; however, it may not be the best choice for a nurse that wants to work in a hospital.

In all of these examples, the interviewers were less likely to take the candidate's answers seriously and were distracted by certain aspects of the candidate's appearance and demeanor that seemed unsuitable for the job. So, my suggestion is to put your personal choices and preferences in fashion, apparel, and accessories aside on the interview day, and follow the simple advice listed below.

Attire and Grooming

Firstly, let us examine some ideas many of us have about dressing for interviews:

Are candidates for all job interviews expected to be dressed "like a CEO" in a suit and tie? Absolutely not.

Does expensive designer apparel make a better first impression? Definitely not.

Is it advisable to dress conservatively for the interview even if the employees wear casual attire to work every day? The answer is yes.

Here are some general tips to make sure your overall appearance is presentable.

- Wear clean, well-fitting clothes.
- Choose clothes in advance and ensure they are ironed.
- If you purchased new clothes for the interview, try them on beforehand.
- Look out for and remove dangling tags and threads.
- Personal hygiene is as essential as attire. Between a well-fitted dress and dirty fingernails, the latter is remembered.
- Use deodorant to mask perspiration but keep it mild. Your perfume should not announce your presence when you walk in.
- Use a mild mouth freshener, as nobody likes the stench of tobacco (in case of smoking), the odor of food or bad breath.
- Do not chew anything such as gum while waiting outside the interview area or during the interview.

Grooming Tips for Men

- Formal pants in muted colors, conservative and well fitting. (Recommended colors are beige, black, blue or gray)

- Plain, check or striped shirt in white or conservative light colors.

- If you choose to wear a tie, pick one with colors that go well with the shirt and a well-formed knot that sits at the neck and does not hang loose.

- Well polished black or brown shoes

- Select a belt of the same color as your shoes without a fancy buckle.

- Make sure to wear socks that are in good condition, without holes or tears. Avoid bold or loud prints and colors. Socks should be long enough so that your legs are not visible while sitting.

- Wear a conservative wristwatch. Avoid wearing a flashy one.

- Your hair should be cut and combed and not disheveled. If sporting a beard, trim it properly.

- Make sure your nails are trimmed and clean.

Grooming Tips for Women

- Wear attire that is considered formal and appropriate for the area/region/country you are interviewing in. The outfit should not be too tight, low cut or too short.

- For western attire consider muted, conservative colors like black, gray, blue, white, beige for skirts and pants and also for jackets and blazers. Shirts and tops can be in light or pastel colors. If you decide to wear local attire, again choose colors that are light and muted and stay away from large, flashy prints.

- Apply light makeup like foundation, lipstick, eyeliner that shows your natural skin tone and complements your eye color. Avoid thick layers of beauty products, very bright and unusual shades of lipstick and stay away from very dark or elaborate eye make-up.

- Clean, trimmed and manicured nails if you so desire, but avoid flashy colors.

- Wear jewelry if you like but again, keep it small – a pair of small earrings, maybe a thin, short necklace with a small pendant. Stay away from very long, heavy, dangling earrings, and large, flashy pendants or rings.

- Keep your hairdo natural and straightforward so that your hair stays out of your eyes and your face is visible. If you apply highlights to your hair, before the interview, apply shades close to your natural hair color.

- Wear comfortable business shoes or sandals with medium size heels that go well with your attire. You may be an expert at standing and walking in stilettos but do you want to risk tripping, stumbling or falling in front of the interviewers?

- Carry a medium size handbag that is not too large or overstuffed and reasonable to hold and carry. The color of the bag should complement the dress and shoes.
- Take care that innerwear is not visible.

Overall, a good rule of thumb is to present yourself such that your appearance does not become the main focus of the interview so your skills, experience, and personality can shine through.

Case Study – Nick and Tony

A large packaging company was conducting interviews for the position of Senior Customer Support Executive. The job involved handling key accounts of large and reputed clients. The selection panel constituted of Senior Management from Marketing, Sales, Quality Assurance, Client Development, and Human Resources.

Two candidates, Nick, and Tony who had applied for the position of Manager of Customer Support were shortlisted by the interview panel and appeared for the final interview. At the end of the day, the interview panel sat down and talked about each candidate they had met.

The VP of sales said, "Look at Tony's profile. I was very impressed with his CV. I thought we had found the guy we wanted, but he kept making a strange face during the interview and didn't look excited about the job. I am not sure anymore." The VP of marketing agreed. "I was very taken aback by his appearance. The way he dressed didn't seem appropriate for a senior level job. His shirt had creases on it, and his tie had a stain. He looked unshaven, and with hair not done. It looked like he got out of bed and rushed to the interview. He has the right qualifications, but I don't recommend him."

The VP of quality assurance chimed in, "I was impressed with Nick. Not only was he confident in his answers, but he also had lots of positive energy. Also, his papers and folders were in order, and although he wasn't wearing a tie, his simple button-down shirt and formal pants were very decent and appropriate." The VP of Marketing weighed in again *"I think he seems to have a better grasp of how to present himself and engage with people and is more likely to succeed at interacting with clients. I recommend that though Nick has less experience than Tony, we select him."*

The VP of HR said, "It sounds like we all agree that Nick was the stronger candidate overall and we should offer him the job." The VP of Marketing sighed, "Oh! What a waste! God help people like Tony."

5
Communication

During your job search, you may have noticed that many listings say "candidate should have excellent communication skills" or "selected candidates will display superior verbal and written communication." Sometimes the ads also specify "looking for individuals who can interact and communicate effectively with clients, team members as well as superiors." It appears as if effective communication is desirable and essential for success in many different jobs.

Take a typical day in your life, from the time you wake up in the morning until you go to bed at night; you engage in many exchanges with different people.

In every aspect of life, from mundane everyday activities to rare, life-altering situations, we have to communicate to make ourselves understood and to understand others. Additionally, the context has a significant impact on how we relate. There is a marked difference between how we speak on the phone versus when we meet a client in person. The latter situation is more formal.

The word communication has roots in the Latin word 'COMMUNIS' which means common. Communication refers to the sharing of ideas, opinions, and information between people and involves not just sending, but also receiving messages and signals through verbal, written or non-verbal means.

In interviews, the importance of communication gets amplified because not only is there limited time, but there is also the stress of being evaluated. For many candidates, these pressures diminish their ability to understand the questions, and they fumble and falter while forming and delivering their replies. As a panelist for interviews, I have seen that ultimately, interviewers picked people that stood out because they communicated more effectively than comparable candidates. In this chapter, I have outlined the characteristics of effective communicators.

The Importance of Listening

Firstly, it is essential to understand that listening is more than just hearing. People that do not listen cannot communicate effectively. Listening is an active process, and it involves

- Giving your full undivided attention to the speakers.
- Showing interest through consistent eye contact.
- Taking notes, if required.
- Not daydreaming – not being lost in thought.
- Focus on the delivery of the message when the speaker is speaking.
- Do not get distracted, fidget, change positions frequently, or look around the room or at the floor.

- Not showing negative expressions and cues while the speaker is talking, e.g., frowning, scowling or grimacing. This indicates, a rejection of the speaker's message.

- Forming your replies in line with what the speakers have said.

- Paraphrasing what is heard – repeating in your own words what the speakers said, to demonstrate your understanding.

- Understanding the "subtext" or the hidden meaning behind the speaker's words.

Advantages of Good Listening

- Good listeners are good leaders.
- Good listeners are good learners.
- Good listeners show interest, empathy and eye contact.
- Good listeners evaluate and prioritize answers.

Finally, good listeners create a great impression.

Good vs. Effective Communication

Good communication entails understanding the content of what one hears, forming and delivering accurate and adequate responses. It requires reasonable command over language and smooth delivery of words and sentences. While good communication abilities are essential, effective communication goes one step further.

Take, for example, anchors of TV shows and news channels. Not only do they deliver information to the public, but they also do it in a way that engages the audience. When you watch your favorite talk show, your attention does not waiver, and you believe what the anchors or the guests are saying because they are charismatic and have an air of confidence. People in public relations, marketing, and publicity roles often succeed because they have learned to communicate in a way that keeps listeners "hooked" to their words. Let me break this down for you.

Clarity and Fluency

I have observed that many candidates have much trouble gathering their thoughts and expressing them clearly and succinctly during interviews even though they have valuable knowledge, experiences, and ideas to share.

A common habit many of us have is using too many filler words such as "like" "you know" "OK" "I mean." In common, filler words and phrases are "so, basically," "actually" "that/this itself" and "haan," "naa." Also, some people take frequent and excessively long pauses and fill them with sounds like "hmm," "uh," "er."

Many candidates say "thank you for that question" after every question. It is not necessary.

Too many extra words, phrases, and sounds make it look like you are delaying your response; either because you do not understand the question, do not have an answer, or you are not confident. On the other hand, talking very fast can also make you appear nervous and impatient.

The importance of "expression" in your voice also cannot be overlooked. Talking in a flat, monotonous style can make you appear bored, and the interviewers may lose interest. Your tone can display a range of emotions – a sense of enthusiasm for your work, pleasure at meeting the interviewers and curiosity about the job and the organization.

Clear and fluent communication entails using the right amount of words, at a medium, relaxed pace, with a sense of comfort and ease.

Persuasiveness

It shows your ability to convince someone of your point of view. When you communicate persuasively, the message is engaging, and it compels listeners to understand, reflect upon and accept your point of view. The listener is impressed and is more likely to agree with your point of view. In jobs that require negotiation, making sales, making deals, settling contracts and dealing with the public, this is an important communication skill.

Assertiveness

It is the ability to express your beliefs, ideas, and thoughts clearly and confidently without ambiguity and is especially crucial in conversations with people with whom you have a difference of opinion. Assertive individuals are forthright; they do not evade difficult conversation. They make decisions quickly and firmly, are comfortable giving directions to others, and like being "in charge."

Assertive individuals use language that has strength and power, but at the same time, are not pushy, aggressive and argumentative. They communicate in a way that reflects decisiveness borne out of firm belief in one's knowledge and experiences.

Non-Verbal Cues

Non-verbal cues come from body language while delivering the message. Looking straight into the eyes of the listeners, not faltering, fidgeting and showing a relaxed disposition has an immense impact on enhancing effectiveness.

I have outlined the essential aspects of communication and how they impact the interview process. Below are some steps you can take to hone your communication skills before the interview day.

- Ask a family member, friend or trusted colleague how they think you are doing on the various aspects of communication outlined in this chapter and what they would suggest you do to improve.

- Take their feedback and suggestions seriously and ask them if they can help you by doing a few practice sessions.

- Go through your CV/resume and practice a few talking points that you can use to explain your significant accomplishments.

- Watch a recording of yourself to self-monitor your volume, speed, tone and also your gestures and facial expressions.

- Look at the sample questions in this book and practice the answers either with a family member, friend or trusted colleague or in front of a mirror before interview day.

6
Applying for a Job

The fact that you are reading this book shows that getting a job you desire is probably a significant target in your life. Like many job seekers, you want more money, responsibility, and respect.

At this stage scanning for job listings in newspapers, job sites and social media is essential. You may come across several openings that are of interest to you. Carefully shortlist those organizations to which you wish to apply.

Now you have to convince hiring organizations to invite you for interviews. This happens only if your profile stands out to hiring committees that usually receive applications from tens, maybe hundreds of hopeful candidates. This chapter will take you through the steps considered vital for your profile to stand out in comparison to other candidates.

Make a Great CV

A Curriculum Vitae also called a CV is a job seeker's most important document. In some professions, a resume, which is a one-page document outlining the course of your career is more common. Both CVs and resumes are snapshots of your career and professional accomplishments and serve important functions for you and the interviewers. For you, your CV is a marketing tool, a first impression before the first impression; your CV precedes you and lands in the hands of the prospective employer before they speak with you or see you. In many organizations, candidates get shortlisted for interviews based on a review of the CVs the hiring committee receives.

Making a CV that stands out goes a long way in ensuring a candidate's success in the interview process. While it is a great idea to spend quality time making your CV, one can also seek assistance from a professional who works with job seekers to design and draft CVs. However, the storyline in the CV has to belong to the job seeker. External assistance will only help in organizing and editing. If you are seeking jobs with more than one organization make sure your CV is tweaked to cater to the job requirements of each organization. So many applications get rejected because their CV was not up to the mark. They had no chance to take a shot at the interview.

Covering Letter

A well-drafted covering letter will enhance the quality and visibility of the CV. Address each covering letter to a specific organization. Please spend some time writing the content of the covering letter and fine-tune it later when you are ready to submit a job application.

Documents and Certificates

Make sure all documents and certificates including any citations and awards, are in order. In most cases, especially in the initial few years of working life, these documents are always needed at the time of interview.

Location/City/Region

All jobs are not in the region or city where the applicant resides. You need to get a general idea where the employment prospects are and be ready to relocate for a new job. Discuss with family and friends to generate consensus.

Compensation

In seeking your first job or changing jobs, the compensation you are looking for is one of the most critical factors. Surveying the current level of compensation will help decide where to apply. Many factors have a bearing on the gross compensation-this may include region, city, general cost of living and industry standards.

Appearance, Attire, and Grooming

Remember the saying 'THE FIRST IMPRESSION IS THE LAST IMPRESSION,' and there is no second chance after the last chance. Chapter four has all the details you need to prepare your appearance, attire, and demeanor before interviews. Think about this early on.

Case Study – XYZ Manufacturing

XYZ manufacturing, a very reputed medium-size engineering company well known for their high-tech products constituted a committee of three midlevel executives to shortlist candidates for a Senior Engineer position for their production lines. The committee included Megha, the Human Resources Manager, Ram, the Technical Manager and Amit, the Production Manager.

The management philosophy at XYZ Manufacturing was to treat their employees with respect and pay them the highest salaries in the industry. XYZ Manufacturing also offered great perquisites and benefits. Lots of young engineers dreamed of working in a place like this.

Megha said, "One of the best ways to understand candidates is to look at their CVs. Has the person taken pains to draft his or her CV according to our job requirements?"

Ram said, "I am a little perplexed. Look at these CVs." He pointed at a bundle kept separately. "These candidates have not taken any pains to down their profile properly. It appears as if they have been copied and pasted from an earlier draft and sent with a changed address."

Amit frowned and said, "There are so many spelling and grammar errors in these CVs." People like these don't stand a chance at getting a significant career break in any reputable organization." Amit added, "I am surprised. Why do they waste their time and ours?"

Megha added, "We see such CVs regularly. Yes, I agree. It's a huge waste of time. We are thinking of blacklisting such profiles. Some of them have repeatedly applied for various posts. We keep a database of all applicants, and in the future, such profiles will not receive any attention."

Megha further added, "But a few CVs here do look good. They are promising candidates. Let us look through these and discuss them."

Finally, the shortlist was made. The quality of the CV and profile were the main criteria. Out of 124 CVs received, only 28 were shortlisted. Fifty-three candidates were rejected solely because their CV's were not up to the mark.

7
The Preliminary Interview

After the application process is complete, if your CV and cover letter make the cut, you will be shortlisted and invited for a preliminary interview, which may be on the telephone, over video, or in some cases in person. You must begin preparing the moment you receive a call asking you to attend the preliminary interview.

The purpose of preliminary interviews is to filter out candidates and to cut short the list to a manageable level. In many cases, a mid-level team member from the division that has the position you applied for, or an HR executive does this interview. In general, the interview focuses on the following.

- Determining a candidate's suitability for the final interview.
- General discussion about the candidate's current job and employment status, compensation expectations and willingness to relocate.
- Insights into why the candidate is applying for this job
- Education and experience.
- Candidate's communication abilities.

Telephone Interview

You will receive communication, which usually comes via email detailing the time and duration of the interview. You are expected to confirm immediately if the date and time work. In case you are not available, state the reason and discuss other time slots. Once a time and date acceptable to both parties are determined, the candidate is expected to be available without distractions with an open and clear phone line.

While preparing for the interview, one must remember that this step is to filter and select candidates for in-person interviews. It would be best if you prepared the questions you may be asked. Also, read the job description and requirements thoroughly and go through your CV. Typically, a tele-interview lasts between 30–45 minutes. This process saves time for both the candidates and the organization and is also a cost-effective method.

At the appointed hour you should

- Be confident as self-assurance gets detected at the other end.
- Keep your CV and other documents within reach.
- When the calls start, greet the caller(s) and thank them for their interest and for giving you this opportunity.
- Speak clearly, without any stress showing in your voice.
- Listen to each question carefully; paraphrase them for clarity.

- Give to-the-point answers, in a confident tone; do not say anything other than the relevant answers.

- Be positive in your responses. Don't criticize anyone especially, your current or former employer(s).

- Speak as if you are sure of becoming one of the candidates to be shortlisted for the final interview.

- Refrain from showing irritation, if you are not clear about a question; do request them to repeat it.

- Speak about your contributions, and how you will bring value to the organization.

At the end of the interview, thank them again for their time and sign off with greetings. Throughout the interview, your tone should convey keenness to work for the organization. Being spontaneous and authentic is important. Remember the people at the other end are very experienced and can detect any stress or hesitation.

Videoconference

All points mentioned in the tele-interview remain valid; also a few more pointers are listed below.

- Make sure you have a stable Internet connection with adequate speed.

- If you are taking this video call from the desk at home, ensure it is clear of clutter.

- The people at the other end can see you, so be well groomed. It is not necessary to wear a suit and tie if the weather does not permit, but formal attire is the best choice.

- Keep a smiling face while answering.

- Do not scowl, frown or make faces.

Case Study – Interview Planning

Reena received an interview call via email just as she entered her house after a day's work. It wasn't unexpected, as she had applied for a job a few days ago.

She had liked the job profile when she came across the advertisement on a popular job site, and she was looking forward to working for this company. She was excited to be shortlisted and to receive an interview call.

She had to make some adjustments in her schedule to be free on the proposed date. After making sure that she was free to attend the interview, she sent out an email to the company confirming her intention to participate in the interview on the proposed date.

Once the date of the interview was confirmed, Reena started planning her trip to the city where she was to attend the interview. The town was two hours away by train and was very well connected. She checked the availability of tickets. Fortunately, tickets for the early morning train were available which would give her enough time to get to the company for her interview. Reena quickly booked her tickets.

She kept her decision about her attire for the coming weekend. That evening, Reena went through the company's website to learn about its products, divisions and more so about the division in which she was seeking the job.

On Friday evening, Reena looked through her dress options. She finalized on a dress and opened it to check if all the buttons were in place. She ironed it again, and also selected one more dress to be kept aside as a backup. She took out a pair of low-heeled sandals that were comfortable and went well with her dress. Then, Reena also kept apart one handbag, which could hold all the things she needed but was not cumbersome to carry. Reena made sure that the purse was of the same color as her shoes. She also took out a folder to carry all her documents.

On Saturday morning, Reena started making notes. She made a list of documents and copies which she needed to bring with her. Once again, Reena checked her tickets to see the departure time, to make arrangements to reach the station in time. Also, she checked on local transport arrangements to reach the venue of the interview.

On Saturday evening, she visited her hairdresser to get a haircut, as she liked to keep her hair short. After the haircut, she trimmed her nails and decided to put light colored nail paint a day before the interview.

8
The Final Interview

Planning and Preparation

One day, you will find in your mailbox a letter inviting you to attend the final interview from an organization you always dreamed of working for! Hoorah!!. Celebrate this moment as you have gotten past one or two levels of shortlisting, and are among the few who will get to take a shot at landing a very coveted job.

Diligent and meticulous preparation must begin now, as success is close! To start, take a look at the calendar to see if any commitments are there. If these are not very urgent, reschedule them. If there is a pressing reason you cannot attend the final interview, communicate immediately with the organization, offer an explanation and ask for alternate dates and times. If you have a genuine reason, most organizations will respond favorably to such requests. As soon as another convenient date and time are available, send a confirmation email and record this in your calendar. If the scheduled interview is in another region, city or town – make travel arrangements as soon as possible.

Now is the time to further hone your communication skills. Look at chapter Five on Communication in this book and implement the practice activities suggested. Remember, practice makes perfect and the more efforts you make to communicate well, the better prepared you will be to speak clearly and with confidence in front of the interview panel. Also, follow the advice on attire and grooming from Chapter Four of this book to present yourself in the best possible light during the interview.

Below is a comprehensive checklist to use for planning and preparation activities. Use this checklist anytime you are interviewing for a new job. Another copy of this checklist is available in Annexure 2 at the end of this book.

Interview Planning and Preparation Checklist

(This checklist is divided into different sections to facilitate proper preparation)

Section 1: General

A. Advertisement/Announcement/Posting

Is a copy of the job advertisement/posting handy? Yes/No

If not, search the source and retrieve it to help you prepare.

B. Interview Call Letter/E-Mail

Have you gone through the details in the posting? Yes/No

Job Title _____

Name of the organization that posted the job:

_____

Dates of interview: _____

Time of interview: _____
(Be careful about time zone, it may be different from where you live)

Address of interview venue: _____

C. Travel Arrangements

Tickets needed?   Yes/No

Travel by: Air/Train/Bus/Driving

Local pick up – To be arranged by you or provided by the organization. (Cross out whichever is not applicable)

Will you require lodging?   Yes/No

Section 2: Knowing the Organization

A. Have you gathered information about the organization?

Division/Department/Section: _____

Major Product/Service Categories: _____

Major Business Segments: _____

Turnover in last three years: _____, _____, _____

Average growth rate: _____%

Public Ltd./Private Ltd./Proprietary

Website URL _____

B. Detailed study of the website

Name of the CEO _____

New Announcements _____, _____, _____

Special achievements if any _____

Other information relevant to your job _____

C. Other information (gleaned from other sources)

Major competition _____, _____, _____

Market share _____

Collaborators/Tie ups _____

Major Customers

Segment wise _____, _____, _____

Section 3: Details about the Job

Skills sought _____, _____,

_____, _____

Experience required: _____

Section 4: Documents

Are all your documents ready?
Yes/No

Do you have photocopies of your documents?
Yes/No

Have you arranged your documents in a folder?
Yes/No

Do you have a copy of your CV (digital/hard copy)?
Yes/No

Section 5: Preparation

Study your CV again and list the main points you would like to emphasize in the upcoming interview that match the job you are applying for.

_____

_____

_____

Anticipating Interview Questions

Any task in which a positive outcome is desired requires a great deal of preparation. Interviews are no different. Now is the time to go over the probable questions and articulate the answers. Remember, one has to be a good salesperson to showcase individual strengths and attributes.

Given below are the types of questions, which I recommend you use for preparation. Find a detailed list of questions in Annexure 1. In addition to these, other questions may crop as a result of discussions you have with the interviewers.

Question Categories

A. Behavioral Questions

These questions form an essential part of any job interview. They are used to get a glimpse of how you conducted yourself in different situations such as situations of stress, disagreement, and instances where you had to make decisions and act under pressure. By knowing how you handled these situations in the past, the interviewers will form an idea of how you're likely to behave as an employee in their organization in the future.

If required pen down your answers and improve them, once you are satisfied with your answers, practice them verbally to boost your confidence. If needed, ask a friend or family member for help.

Your answers must be short and to the point. Very verbose and lengthy statements will make you look confused. In many cases, answering such behavioral questions in a storytelling manner to narrate the instance and your role in it impresses the interviewers. Look at the section on Answering Style in the next chapter for more details.

B. Traditional Questions

These questions are relatively straightforward and are asked to gain more information about the candidate. Usually, your CV will be the reference used for asking these questions. These open-ended questions typically cover some of the following areas of candidates' interests and past experiences.

- Planning, scheduling, and organizing
- Leadership
- Teamwork
- Initiative and drive
- Strengths
- Weaknesses

- Choices and actions
- Goals
- Motives

The Day before the Interview

Your interview is tomorrow. Here are some things you could spend some time today to help you feel confident and ready.

- Have you put together a few storylines that you can tell about some of the achievements and skills you have listed on your CV?
- Can you answer questions about your CV?
- Have you researched the organization thoroughly?
- Make sure that all your documents are in order.
- Have you gone through potential questions and practiced your responses?
- What about your dress and attire?
- Have you made up your mind regarding the need to relocate if the job requires?
- Have you determined your salary and compensations expectations?
- Perform some breathing exercises, meditate or do other things to get as relaxed as possible.
- Make sure you have a good night's sleep.

Social Media

In today's world, social media is an essential source of information. A large number of organizations do search social media to understand the candidates.

You may own several social media accounts on Facebook, LinkedIn, and Twitter. Make sure that you mention any professional social networks you are part of in your CV. Do take care of what you have posted, your feeds and your likes. People understand your worldview from what you subscribe to and your activities on social media.

Also ensure that you regularly post important events where you have demonstrated your leadership as well as your participation in areas relevant to your profession, education and social standing. These do create a great impression of you. Avoid controversies; they are not helpful at all.

Do not be surprised if the interviewers ask you some questions related to your activities on social media; in fact, it will show their interest in who you are, your opinions, contributions, and achievements.

9
Handling the Final Interview

The moment that you have been waiting for has come. Today is your interview for the dream job that you have always wanted. If you have done what I have advised in this book, you can hope for a very positive outcome.

All your preparation so far has brought you to this make-or-break step of the interview process. The insights written below will empower you to give your best performance at this critical juncture.

Starting Right

Start your day well. Make sure you attend to your dress and grooming. Also, be sure of the route to the venue and transport arrangements to reach in time.

Organize your documents folder or file well and neatly file all your papers so that they do not slip or fly out. If this happens, you will look very clumsy.

When you reach the venue, greet the organization officials warmly. They will usher you to a room and ask you to be seated to wait for your turn. Let them know your return transport timings.

Usually, each candidate is given an interview time slot, but there may be a delay, as interviews with other candidates sometimes do not finish in time. By letting them know your return travel timings, they will ensure that your interview time is advanced.

In case you notice other candidates waiting in the room, greet them as well. Switch off your cell phone, remain relaxed and wait your turn.

Your Turn Now

Someone walks up to you and guides you to the interview room. Collect your papers, stride confidently and keep a relaxed face. Your interview begins the moment you come within sight of the interview panel.

What Do You Do Now?

- Greet the interviewers with a clear voice; look straight into their eyes.
- Shake hands confidently
- Wait to be seated.

Once you are seated, thank them. Also, thank everyone for the interview opportunity and wait expectantly for the first question. Don't fidget, wring your hands or shake your legs but present an alert, confident and positive posture.

The Interview Begins

Listen to the question; wait for the whole question to be stated. Look at the person who is asking the question, nod to convey your understanding, paraphrase if necessary.

Now answer; your voice should be clear and audible, but not very loud. Structure your answer carefully. Look at the individuals who had asked the question, but also glance at others.

Make sure the answer is specific to the question; don't bring extraneous points, which may not be relevant. It will distract the interviewers, and they won't like it. After all, they already have a line of questioning in their minds to ascertain your suitability. Also, such distractions may create openings for questions, for which you are not prepared.

Most of the questions will be from what you have written in your CV, the application form, and the requirements in the job advertisement. It would be best if you had also prepared along the same lines so stick to the script.

Selling Yourself

Personal interviews are all about selling yourself. If you can't sell your self, no one else can. Be ready to answer the questions authentically.

There may be some things you may not know, say that also with confidence. Admitting that you don't know some things makes you appear honest, transparent and human, as no one on earth knows everything.

The Most Suitable Person

Answer in a manner that the interviewers begin to think that you are the most suitable person for the job and you will contribute significantly towards one or more of the following

- Improving business performance.
- Enhancing profitability.
- Improving the organization's image.
- Problem-solving.
- Innovation and out-of-the-box thinking.
- Leadership.
- Adaptability and flexibility.

Drive, Initiative, and Energy

Interviewers are looking for candidates who have drive and energy to take on challenges and show results. After all, an organization faces rapid changes in the business environment, and they need individuals with the initiative and capacity to handle such changes competently.

Answering Style

Speak in a manner that conveys you believe in your words. A storytelling style is also useful because it captures the imagination of the listeners. Then they will begin to think that by losing you they will be losing too much. Use the following framework to tell a story of how you effectively solved a problem in a previous job:

- Introduce a specific incident, situation or problem that arose.
- Describe the situation briefly.

- Give your assessment of the problem.
- Explain what you did.
- Describe the results.

The above approach always does the trick. You will find the listeners leaning forward, listening intently, nodding their heads and sending glances of approval to each other. Everyone likes to hear a story, and you will have taken the interviewers through some of your stories scene-by-scene. Then, follow-up questions will be asked only to seek clarification.

Questions from the Candidate

During most interviews, candidates have an opportunity to ask questions. Preparing your questions in advance is crucial. Your questions can cover one or more of the following areas

- The kind of job and work you are expected to do
- The division, department and the reporting relationships
- Plans and development concerning your field of work
- Growth Plans, Investments, Market Share, New Product Development, Collaboration, Tie-Ups, and Technology Upgrades.

Do not ask questions about only your compensation and perquisites because that will show you are only interested in salary and benefits, and not in your job and career prospects. Also, not asking any questions is not a good sign as it reflects your disinterest or lack of preparation for the interview.

Interview Closure

The moment the questions and discussions come to an end, you will receive a polite indication that the interview is over and you will hear from them shortly. Keep smiling; shake hands all around, and collect your documents in an orderly manner. Thank the interviewers for their time and stride out confidently.

As you leave, do thank the person who handled your arrival, don't linger around. Do not forget to send a thank you note immediately to the Human Resources department or the individual who sent you a call for the interview. It is a good gesture.

Handling Difficult Situations

1. Not reaching in time
   unless you are stuck because of an emergency, you will find great difficulty in explaining why this happened.

2. Papers falling as you arrive in the room
   Look straight into the eyes of the panel and apologize for being untidy. If all goes well during your interview, this will be soon forgotten.

3. Not asked to be seated
   Wait, keep standing near the chair, keep a smiling face, someone is testing you, soon you will be requested to take your seat.

4. Distraction
   Someone from the panel is doing other work, sending a text or attending a call. Wait patiently.

5. Mobile phones
   Keep these in silent mode (non-buzz) or switched off to avoid distraction.

6. Tea/Snack service
   Accept politely, don't let your tea go cold (if you don't drink tea or coffee say so and ask for water if you want), don't spill in the saucer. Don't make noise while drinking or eating. Don't speak with your mouth full.

7. What are your weaknesses?
   This question is difficult to handle. No human is without weakness, and you are no exception. When you answer, tell the panel about how you have tried to overcome your weakness.

8. Why are you looking for a change? Why did you leave your last job?
   Don't tell them that the company was terrible or the boss was a tyrant, all bosses are.

9. What are your strengths?
   Don't brag; give a few examples of how you have used your strengths to make positive contributions in your previous job(s).

10. Why should we hire you?
    Again don't brag or say that you are the best on the earth. Tell them how you will contribute towards meeting the organization's goals, improve its growth and be an asset to them.

11. Questions about the future – where do you want to be in 5 years/10 years?
    It is a tricky question to answer. Tell about your career plans and life goals. A candidate who thinks about the future and has clarity about what he or she wants impresses.

12. Tell us about yourself.
    Don't talk about any fancy activities but speak about your specific skills and achievements. Do tell the panel about your value system and why they are important to you. Tell them about your interests and hobbies. Let them know how you took leadership or participated in projects or activities.

Group Discussion

For newly graduated individuals, group discussions are an essential step in the selection process. Life is all about working together. In your professional life, you will meet several people like customers, suppliers, peers, and colleagues from different disciplines and departments. Your ability to contribute positively to interactions, meetings, and discussions is critical. In the workplace, no two days are the same, and you will have to react intelligently to emerging situations.

While grades from universities and schools are an indication of scholastic abilities, during group discussion the skills of an individual to articulate, dialogue and effectively communicate are exposed. It is during group discussions that the interviewers gauge your capabilities for quick thinking and giving reasoned responses.

Group Discussion Skills (G.D)

Excellent communication skills including listening abilities are the backbone of good G.D skills. Some important to-dos are:

- Intervening at the right moment.
- Effectively delivering your point of view,
- Using language that is engaging and persuasive.
- Speaking in a manner that compels others to think.
- Using time well.
- Showing interest and attention to other participants' points of view.

G.D Preparation

The topic for a group discussion is rarely given in advance. After the announcement of the topic, you need to think fast and respond. Time is of great essence, so get ready quickly with an initial response and speak rationally and coherently. Below are some essential tips for G.D.

- **Evaluate:** Quickly evaluate and understand the core of the topic. You have only a few minutes. Make notes if required.

- **Decide:** Decide your opening arguments and reasoning to support them.

- **Speak:** Articulate your points in proper order.

- **Imagine:** As you speak, imagine the responses you will get to the points you are making. Be ready to counter them. This way you will remain one step ahead.

- **Emotions:** Control your emotions. Remember you are participating in a G.D. If you don't agree with other participants' points of view, don't appear upset or angry, and never raise your voice.

G.D. is used to judge candidates' ability to think on their feet. To identify who has fresh ideas and can think differently. Individuals who are looking for jobs after graduation are strongly advised to participate in a few group discussions while they are in college. Not being able to handle a group discussion can lead to immediate rejection.

Body Language

Don't clench fists, shake your legs, and make threatening gestures. Remain alert, make eye contact, pace your words well and speak with a firm tone.

Interventions

Make at least 3 to 4 interventions in a 20 to 25-minute G.D. session. Don't repeat yourself.

Listening

Listen to what others are saying; look for support for your viewpoints.

Leadership

Look for opportunities to lead and open the discussion. Summarize, what you have said. Emphasize the core points of your perspective.

Post Interview Reflections

Your interview is over, and you are going back. You still do not know the outcome. Sometimes the wait can be agonizing. Once you are back home, it is natural that you are mulling over what happened during the interview. You are not alone; nearly everyone goes through this. I recommend that you spend some quality time reflecting upon how you fared during the interview.

I also recommend that you make notes of your reflections, as you are the first and the best judge of how you fared during the interview. Your notes will not only help you to pen your thoughts but also be of great use to you to do better next time.

An excellent way to do this is to make notes under two headings given below.

I. What Went Well?

Think about which aspects of the interview you handled well.

- Think about those questions for which you had spontaneous responses.

- Think about instances when you communicated well.

- Think about the questions for which you received positive responses or cues.

- Try to recall responses that generated the interviewers 'interest, and they wanted to know more.

- What do you think about the overall impression you created?

- How well prepared were you for the interview?

- Which parts of the checklist did you prepare well? Did that help?

- Out of the questions listed in the Annexure(s), which ones did you work on? Did this preparation help you?

II. What Could Be Better?

Try to recall questions or instances where you felt you did not answer well or your preparation was not up to the mark.

- How was your communication? Could it be better? Did you need more practice?
- Did you leave any part of the checklist unattended and do you think it showed in your performance?
- Out of the list of questions, were there any questions you had not prepared and did they crop up?
- Did you demonstrate active listening to the questions?
- Did you ensure that you spoke to the point?
- Did you come across as aggressive or overconfident?
- Did you notice interviewers frowning or grimacing in response to your answers?
- Were you satisfied with your grooming and attire?

In addition to the above, write down any other points you remember. The quicker you sit down to reflect the better it will be as your memory is still fresh and you can visualize correctly. Put all your notes as an attachment in this book for you to review next time, even if you are selected.

Annexure 1
Behavioral Interview Questions

Given below is a comprehensive list of Behavioral Interview Questions. The panel may not ask all the questions listed here, but they are available for you to prepare thoroughly.

Teamwork

1. Describe a situation when you excelled as a team member.

2. Describe how you handled disagreements in the team.

3. Please describe how you dealt with team members not doing their share of work.

4. Describe what you have learned by being a team member.

5. What difficulties have you have faced being part of a team?

6. Describe your actions to build consensus among team members.

7. Describe how you handled situations when other team. members did not accept your point of view even when you were right.

Adaptability

1. Tell us how you adjusted to your superiors' working style.

2. Tell us how you adjusted to changes in the work environment over which you had no control?

Problem-Solving

1. Tell us about the most challenging situation in your work life and how you dealt with it.

2. How do you generally approach a problem? Outline the steps.

3. Describe to us if you have resolved a problem creatively.

4. Tell us three improvements you have made in your work areas in the preceding six months.

5. What methods have you adopted to anticipate problems and to prevent them?

6. After the resolution of a problem, what steps did you take to ensure that it did not reoccur?

7. Tell us about the most innovative new idea you have implemented so far.

8. What was the most challenging problem you came across, why did you consider it most difficult and how did you solve it?

9. What steps did you follow to analyze a problem and suggest solutions?

10. Did you come across a problem situation that jeopardized the safety and security of the organization and people? How did you correct the situation?

11. Are you in the habit of using specific tools for problem identification, analysis and solving? Can you elaborate what these are?

Communication

1. Did you come across a situation when you had to sell an idea to your management? What steps did you take?

2. Have you come across a situation when others did not agree with your point of view, even though you were right? How did you handle this situation?

3. What difficulties have you faced in communicating your viewpoints to your superiors and how did you overcome them?

4. What method(s) of communication have you adopted to convey to your colleague's urgent job requirements?

5. How did you communicate with your subordinate(s) that their performance is below par without demotivating them?

Initiative

1. Describe an idea, plan or improvement implemented because of your initiative.

2. What initiatives did you start to improve work and performance in your areas of responsibility?

3. What new initiatives have you taken up to develop the people who work with you?

4. Describe initiatives you started to improve work culture.

5. What specific initiatives did you start to enhance teamwork?

6. What initiatives have you taken to improve financial performance?

7. Tell us about the steps taken by you in making use of technology and improved methods?

8. What initiatives have you taken to improve your knowledge and capability?

Leadership

1. Tell us about an important project you led. Outline your leadership role.

2. In general, what are the specific methods used by you to motivate your team where you found yourself placed in a leadership role?

3. What are the biggest obstacles you have faced as a leader?

4. Have you undertaken any leadership activity outside your work area?

5. What has been your significant learning as a team leader?

6. Describe your role as a leader in taking your team together to achieve what seemed like an impossible goal.

7. Define in your words the role of a leader.

8. Tell us, how have you handled reluctant and difficult team members?

9. Have you led a problem-solving project or activity? What was it? Describe your leadership role.

Time Management, Planning, and Organizing

1. Tell us how do you handle the pressures of your day.

2. When faced with a situation of doing several things at the same time, how do you organize?

3. Please tell us how you organize and schedule your tasks to complete a project or an activity.

4. Have you had a situation when an activity or project did not go as per plan? If yes, what did you learn from it?

5. On what basis do you prioritize your tasks?

6. How frequently do you review goals and how do you take corrective action?

Client/Customer Interaction Skills

1. Give us an example of exceptional customer service or support you delivered.

2. Give us an example of how you convinced a customer to favor your company when they were always loyal to the competitor.

3. Have you come across an agitated customer? Tell us how you handled the situation.

4. Out of many competing needs, how did you go about prioritizing customer(s) needs?

5. Have you had an occasion where you had to defend a customer to your management? How did you go about doing it?

6. What in your opinion is customer satisfaction?

7. What in your opinion is customer delight?

Decision-Making

1. How do you rate your decision-making?

2. To you, what are the most important considerations when making decisions?

3. How have you conveyed decisions that may be unpalatable to some?

4. Give examples of decisions you took that have been implemented by your organization(s)?

5. Give examples of decisions you made that had a positive impact.

6. When do you think the collaborative style of decision-making works best?

7. Narrate an instance when a decision taken by you went wrong.

Interpersonal Skills

1. Give us insight(s) on how you dealt with someone who was difficult to get along?.

2. Have you faced a situation when someone did not like you, but you had to deal with that person? How did you do that?

3. In case of conflict between your division and another division, how did you go about finding an acceptable resolution?

4. Have you come across a situation where there was a language or understanding barrier? How did you handle that situation?

5. How did you develop trust with colleagues and peers?

6. How do you create rapport with people?

Other Behavioral Questions

1. Tell us something about yourself
2. What is your greatest strength?
3. What are your weaknesses?
4. Why should we hire you?
5. What are you expecting from this job?
6. What are the values you cherish most?
7. What motivates you in life?
8. Talk about a time when you wanted to do something but failed to do so.
9. Tell us about an instance when you performed to the best of your capabilities.
10. Talk about a situation where you learned from your own mistakes.
11. When you faced difficulty convincing someone of your point of view, what did you do?
12. Describe a situation when you were able to motivate someone to perform better.
13. What do you know about this organization?
14. Would you be able to do this job well?
15. Which of your skills will benefit our organization?
16. What do you expect from a good superior?

17. How will you handle a tough and demanding superior?

18. Describe a situation when you helped your group to resolve conflict and reach consensus.

19. Please tell us how you handle work stress and mounting demands.

20. How have you used the skills of your subordinates for the organization's benefit?

21. Please tell us what makes you trust people.

22. Tell us how you identified skills, and distributed and delegated work?

Annexure 2
Interview Planning and Preparation Checklist

(This checklist is divided into different sections to facilitate proper preparation)

Section 1: General

A. Advertisement/Announcement/Posting

Is a copy of the job advertisement/posting handy? Yes/No

If not, search the source and retrieve it to help you prepare.

B. Interview Call Letter/E-Mail

Have you gone through the details in the posting? Yes/No

Job Title _____

Name of the organization that posted the job:

_____

Dates of interview: _____

Time of interview: _____
(Be careful about time zone, it may be different from where you live)

Address of interview venue: _____

C. Travel Arrangements

Tickets needed?   Yes/No

Travel by: Air/Train/Bus/Driving

Local pick up – To be arranged by you or provided by the organization. (Cross out whichever is not applicable)

Will you require lodging?   Yes/No

Section 2: Knowing the Organization

A. Have you gathered information about the organization?

Division/Department/Section: _____

Major Product/Service Categories: _____

Major Business Segments: _____

Turnover in last three years: _____, _____, _____

Average growth rate: _____%

Public Ltd./Private Ltd./Proprietary

Website URL _____

B. Detailed study of the website

Name of the CEO _____

New Announcements _____, _____, _____

Special achievements if any _____

Other information relevant to your job _____

C. Other information (gleaned from other sources)

Major competition _____, _____, _____

Market share _____

Collaborators/Tie ups _____

Major Customers

Segment wise _____, _____, _____

Section 3: Details about the Job

Skills sought _____, _____,

_____, _____

Experience required: _____

Section 4: Documents

Are all your documents ready?
Yes/No

Do you have photocopies of your documents?
Yes/No

Have you arranged your documents in a folder?
Yes/No

Do you have a copy of your CV (digital/hard copy)?
Yes/No

Section 5: Preparation

Study your CV again and list the main points you would like to emphasize in the upcoming interview that match the job you are applying for.

_____

_____

_____

www.ingramcontent.com/pod-product-compliance
Lightning Source LLC
Chambersburg PA
CBHW030915180526
45163CB00004B/1844